Chicken Breast Recipes

Chef Leonardo

Chicken Breast Recipes

Copyright © 2021 Chef Leonardo

© Chef Leonardo 2021 - All rights reserved by the author. No part of this book may be reproduced without prior permission of the author.

No part of this document may be reproduced, duplicated or transmitted in any way in digital or printed form. The distribution of this publication is strictly prohibited and any use of this document is not permitted without the prior written consent of the publisher. All rights reserved.

It is guaranteed the accuracy and integrity of the information contained in this document, but no kind of responsibility is assumed. It is the sole and absolute responsibility of the intended reader, in terms of misinterpretation of the information through carelessness or the use or misuse of any policies, processes or instructions contained within the book. Under no circumstances may the publisher be prosecuted or blamed for any damage done or monetary loss incurred as a result of information contained in this book, either directly or indirectly.

The rights are owned by the respective authors and not by the publisher.

Legal notice: This book is protected by copyright. It is for personal use only. You may not modify, distribute, sell, use, quote or paraphrase any part of the contents of this book without the specific consent of the author or owner of the copyright.

In accordance with the law.

Disclaimer:

Please note that the contents of this book are for educational and entertainment purposes only.

Table Of Content

1. Parsley and Chicken Breast 5
2. Shredded Chicken Taco Filling 8
3. Herb-Roasted Chicken Breasts.............. 12
4. Rice and Chicken Soup 16
5. Chicken Sandwich 20
6. Chicken Fajitas 22
7. Chicken with Rosemary-Garlic Sauce 26
8. Chicken Paprika 30
9. Grilled Chicken Marsala 33
10. Classic Chicken Soup 37
11. Imond Chicken................................... 41
12. Chicken and Mushroom Stew................ 44
13. Blackened Chicken 47
14. Grilled Chicken Salad.......................... 51
15. Chicken with Mushroom Sauce 54
16. Creamy Chicken with Cider 58
17. Chicken Kebab Sandwich 61
18. Aromatic Chicken and Cabbage Stir-Fry ..64
19. Thai-Style Chicken Curry 67

Chicken Breast Recipes

20. Chicken Satay with Peanut Sauce 71
21. Chicken Breast and Bok Choy in Parchment 75
22. Chicken, Pasta, and Broccoli Bake 79
23. Chicken Pho 83
24. Curried Chicken Stir-Fry 86
25. Creamy Chicken 90
26. Fabulous Chicken 93
27. Chicken with Asian Vegetables 97

1. Parsley and Chicken Breast

Preparation Time: 10 minutes

Cooking Time: 40 minutes

Servings: 4

Ingredients:

- 1 tablespoon dry parsley
- 1 tablespoon dry basil
- 4 chicken breast halves, boneless and skinless
- 1/2 teaspoon salt
- 1/2 teaspoon red pepper flakes, crushed

Chicken Breast Recipes

Directions:

1. Preheat your oven to 350 °F

2. Take a 9x13 inch baking dish and grease it with cooking spray

3. Sprinkle 1 tablespoon of parsley, 1 teaspoon of basil and spread the mixture over your baking dish

4. Arrange the chicken breast halves over the dish and sprinkle garlic slices on top

5. Take a small bowl and add 1 teaspoon parsley, 1 teaspoon of basil, salt, basil, red pepper and mix well. Pour the mixture over the chicken breast

6. Bake for 25 minutes

7. Remove the cover and bake for 15 minutes more

8. Serve and enjoy!

Nutrition: Calories: 150 Fat: 4g Carbohydrates: 4g Protein: 25g

Chicken Breast Recipes

Note:

2. Shredded Chicken Taco Filling

Chicken Breast Recipes

Preparation Time: 15 minutes

Cooking Time: 15 minutes

Servings: 10

Ingredients:

- 2 - cups diced onions
- 2 ¼ - pounds boneless, skinless chicken breast
- ½ - cup lime juice
- 1 - teaspoon ground coriander
- 2 ½ - teaspoons cumin
- 2 - teaspoons garlic powder
- 1 - Tablespoon smoked paprika
- 1 ½ - teaspoon chili powder

Directions:

1. With cooking oil try spray the side and bottom of a cooker.
2. Spot onions on the base of the slight cooker; include chicken, lime squeeze and flavors.
3. Cook on LOW for 8hrs or until the hen is completed;
4. Shred chook with 2 forks.

Chicken Breast Recipes

5.   It can serve on flour tortillas and top with lettuce and sharp cream (optional).

Nutrition: Calories: 117 Fat: 3g Protein: 22g Carbs: 5g

Chicken Breast Recipes

Note:

3. Herb-Roasted Chicken Breasts

Preparation Time: 10 minutes

Cooking Time: 30 minutes

Servings: 4

Ingredients:

- 1-pound boneless, skinless chicken breasts
- 1 medium onion

Chicken Breast Recipes

- 1–2 garlic cloves
- 2 tablespoons Mrs. Dash® Garlic and Herb Seasoning Blend
- 1 teaspoon ground black pepper
- ¼ cup olive oil

Directions:

1. Marinating:
2. Chop onion and garlic and place in a bowl. Add Mrs. Dash Seasoning, ground pepper and olive oil.
3. Add chicken breasts to the marinade, cover it, then refrigerate for at least 4 hours or overnight.

Baking:

4. Preheat the oven to 350°F.
5. Cover a baking sheet with foil, place the marinated chicken breasts on the pan.
6. Pour the remaining marinade over the chicken and bake at 350°F for 20 minutes.
7. Broil an additional 5 minutes for browning.

Nutrition: Calories: 270 kcal Total Fat: 17 g Saturated Fat: 3 g Cholesterol: 83 mg Sodium: 53

mg Total Carbs: 3 g fibre: 0 g Sugar: 0 g Protein: 26 g

Chicken Breast Recipes

Note:

4. Rice and Chicken Soup

Preparation Time: 7 minutes

Cooking Time: 20 minutes

Servings: 8

Ingredients:

- 1 cup white onion, finely chopped
- 1 cup celery, diced
- 2 tbsp Extra virgin oil

Chicken Breast Recipes

- 1 cup baby carrot, chopped
- ½ tsp fresh ground black pepper
- ¾ cup instant white rice
- 1 bay leaf
- 4 fresh thyme sprigs
- 2 boneless skinless chicken breasts, cooked and cubed
- 10 cups no salt added chicken/vegetable broth
- 2 tbsp lime juice

Directions:

1. Sauté celery, carrot, and onion in olive oil in a large pot. Cook until softened.
2. Cook rice.
3. Add pepper, fresh thyme, bay leaf, rice, and stock. Bring to a boil.
4. Reduce heat and let simmer for 15 minutes.
5. Add chicken and cook ten minutes more.
6. Add lime juice.
7. Remove Bay leaf before serving.

Nutrition: Protein -14g Carbohydrates - 19g Fat - 3g Calories – 160

Chicken Breast Recipes

Note:

5. Chicken Sandwich

Preparation Time: 10 minutes

Cooking Time: 20 minutes

Servings: 2

Ingredients:

- 2 pieces Boston leaf lettuce
- 1.4 oz chicken breast, grilled and cooled
- 1 green onion, sliced
- ½ cup seedless grapes, halved
- 1 tbsp low-fat mayonnaise
- ½ cup celery, diced

Chicken Breast Recipes

- ¼ tsp cinnamon
- 1 tbsp lemon juice
- 1 cup of fresh basil leaves
- 2 slices white bread, toasted

Directions:

1. Combine all ingredients except lettuce, basil, and bread in a large bowl.

2. Spread a small amount of the mixture over toast and top with basil.

3. Place Boston lettuce leaf on top and serve.

Nutrition: Protein - 20g Carbohydrates - 20g Fat - 6g Calories – 220

6. Chicken Fajitas

Chicken Breast Recipes

Preparation Time: 10 minutes

Cooking Time: 10 minutes

Servings: 8

Ingredients:

- 8 flour tortillas, 6" size
- 1/4 cup green pepper, cut in strips
- 1/4 cup red pepper, cut in strips
- 1/2 cup onion, sliced
- 1/2 cup cilantro
- 2 tbsp canola oil
- 12 oz boneless chicken breasts
- 1/4 tsp black pepper
- 2 tsp chili powder
- 1/2 tsp cumin
- 2 tbsp lemon juice

Directions:

1. Start by wrapping the tortillas in a foil.

2. Warm them up for 10 minutes in a preheated oven at 300 degrees F.

3. Add oil to a non-stick pan.

4. Add lemon juice chicken and seasoning.

5. Stir fry for 5 minutes then add onion and peppers.

6. Continue cooking for 5 minutes or until chicken is tender.

7. Stir in cilantro, mix well, and serve in tortillas.

Nutrition: Calories 343. Protein 24 g. Carbohydrates 33 g. Fat 13 g. Cholesterol 53 mg. Sodium 281 mg. Potassium 331 mg. Phosphorus 196 mg. Calcium 23 mg. Fibre 2.0 g.

Chicken Breast Recipes

Note:

7. Chicken with Rosemary-Garlic Sauce

Chicken Breast Recipes

Preparation Time: 10 minutes

Cooking Time: 20 minutes

Servings: 8

Ingredients:

- 2 cups low-sodium chicken broth
- 1/2 cup balsamic vinegar
- 1/2 cup white wine
- 1 tbsp fresh rosemary, chopped
- 8 boneless, skinless chicken breasts
- 1 head garlic clove, chopped
- 2 tbsp olive or canola oil
- 1/8 teaspoon black pepper, to taste

Directions:

1. Start by mixing the wine, rosemary, broth, and vinegar in a 9x13 inch baking pan.
2. Place the chicken breasts in it and rub the marinade into the meat. Marinate overnight.
3. Grease a saucepan with oil and add garlic.
4. Sauté until golden then set the garlic aside.
5. Season the marinated chicken with black pepper and sear it for 5 minutes per side until golden.

Chicken Breast Recipes

6. Pour the reserved marinade over it along with garlic.

7. Cook on reduced heat for 15 minutes and flip the chicken after 7 minutes.

8. Transfer the chicken to the serving plates.

9. Cook the remaining liquid until it thickens into a sauce.

10. Pour the sauce over the chicken.

11. Serve warm and fresh.

Nutrition: Calories 210. Protein 28 g. Carbohydrates 4 g. Fat 7 g. Cholesterol 70 mg. Sodium 85 mg. Potassium 277 mg. Phosphorus 208 mg. Calcium 26 mg. Fibre 0.2 g.

Chicken Breast Recipes

Note:

8. Chicken Paprika

Preparation Time: 10 minutes

Cooking Time: 1 hour 35 minutes

Servings: 6

Ingredients:

- 2 tbsp canola oil
- 1/2 cup onion, finely chopped
- 1 tbsp sweet Hungarian paprika
- 1/2 tsp black pepper
- 6 chicken breasts, bone-in

Chicken Breast Recipes

- 2 cups of water
- Cooking spray
- 1 cup reduced-fat sour cream

Directions:

1. Start by greasing a large pan with canola oil.

2. Add onion and sauté until golden.

3. Add pepper and paprika for seasoning,

4. Place the chicken in the pan and sauté well for 5 minutes.

5. Add water and then cover the pan with a suitable lid.

6. Let chicken simmer covered for 1.5 hours on low heat.

7. Stir in sour cream and mix well.

8. Serve warm and fresh.

Nutrition: Calories 267. Protein 30 g. Carbohydrates 3 g. Fat 15 g. Cholesterol 94 mg. Sodium 176 mg. Potassium 328 mg. Phosphorus 253 mg. Calcium 63 mg. Fibre 0.6 g.

Chicken Breast Recipes

Note:

9. Grilled Chicken Marsala

Preparation Time: 10 minutes

Cooking Time: 20 minutes

Servings: 4

Ingredients:

- 1/3 cup unsalted butter
- 1/2 oz sliced prosciutto, diced
- 2 tsp shallots, minced
- 2 tsp garlic, minced
- 1/2 cup fresh mushrooms, sliced

Chicken Breast Recipes

- 1/4 cup Marsala wine
- 1-1/4 tsp ground black pepper
- 1 cup low-sodium chicken broth
- 2 tsp cornstarch - 1 tsp fresh parsley, minced
- 2 tbsp heavy cream
- 1/2 tsp dried oregano - 1/2 tsp dried thyme
- 1/2 tsp dried parsley - 1/4 tsp marjoram
- 1/4 tsp garlic powder - 1/4 tsp onion powder
- 4 boneless, skinless chicken breasts - 2 tbsp olive oil

Directions:

1. Warm the butter in a saucepan over low heat.
2. Add prosciutto and sauté for 3 minutes.
3. Stir in shallots and garlic to sauté for another 30 seconds.
4. Now, add Marsala wine and stir fry for 30 seconds.

5. Add mushrooms and black pepper then cook for 5 minutes on a simmer.

6. Mix the corn-starch with broth in a bowl and pour it into the saucepan stirring to incorporate it.

7. Cook for 5 minutes then add parsley and cream.

8. Cover the pan and let it cook for 4 minutes until it thickens.

9. Meanwhile, season the chicken with the remaining spices and herbs liberally.

10. Wrap it in a plastic wrap and pound it with a mallet. Rub the chicken with the oil.

11. Now, preheat a grill on medium heat and grill the chicken breast for 8 minutes per side.

12. Slice the grilled chicken and serve with the Marsala sauce on top. Enjoy with freshly cooked pasta.

Nutrition: Calories 581. Protein 36 g. Carbohydrates 44 g. Fat 29 g. Cholesterol 125 mg. Sodium 392 mg. Potassium 441 mg. Phosphorus 318 mg. Calcium 55 mg. Fibre 1.6 g.

… Chicken Breast Recipes

Note:

10. Classic Chicken Soup

Preparation Time: 5-10 minutes

Cooking Time: 35 minutes

Serving: 1

Ingredients:

- 2 teaspoons minced garlic
- 2 celery stalks, chopped

Chicken Breast Recipes

- 1 tablespoon unsalted butter
- ½ sweet onion, diced
- 1 carrot, diced
- 4 cups of water
- 1 teaspoon chopped fresh thyme
- 2 cups chopped cooked chicken breast
- 1 cup chicken stock
- 1/8 teaspoon black pepper (ground), to taste
- 2 tablespoons chopped fresh parsley

Directions:

1. Take a medium-large cooking pot, heat oil over medium heat.
2. Add onion and stir-cook until it becomes translucent and softened.
3. Add garlic and stir-cook until it becomes fragrant.
4. Add celery, carrot, chicken, chicken stock, and water.
5. Boil the mixture.
6. Over low heat, simmer the mixture for about 25-30 minutes until veggies are tender.

7. Mix in thyme and cook for 2 minutes. Season to taste with black pepper.

8. Serve warm with parsley on top.

Nutrition (Per Serving): Calories: 135 Fat: 6g Phosphorus: 122mg Potassium: 208mg Sodium: 74mg Carbohydrates: 3g Protein: 15g.

Chicken Breast Recipes

Note:

11. lmond Chicken

Preparation Time: 15 minutes

Cooking Time: 15 minutes

Serving: 3

Ingredients:

- 2 large chicken breasts, boneless and skinless
- 1/3 cup lemon juice
- 1 ½ cups seasoned almond meal
- 2 tablespoons coconut oil
- 1/8 teaspoon lemon pepper, to taste

- Parsley for decoration

Directions:

1. Slice chicken breast in half

2. Pound out each half until ¼ inch thick

3. Take a pan and place over medium heat, add oil and heat it up

4. Dip each chicken breast slice into lemon juice and let it sit for 2 minutes

5. Turnover and let the other side sit for 2 minutes as well

6. Transfer to almond meal and coat both sides

7. Add coated chicken to the oil and fry for 4 minutes per side, making sure to sprinkle lemon pepper liberally

8. Transfer to a paper-lined sheet and repeat until all chicken is fried

9. Garnish with parsley and enjoy!

Nutrition: Calories: 325 Fat: 24g Carbohydrates: 3g Protein: 16g

Chicken Breast Recipes

Note:

12. Chicken and Mushroom Stew

Preparation Time: 10 minutes

Cooking Time: 35 minutes

Serving: 4

Ingredients:

- 4 chicken breast halves, cut into bite-sized pieces
- 1-pound mushrooms, sliced (5-6 cups)
- 1 bunch spring onion, chopped
- 4 tablespoons olive oil
- 1 teaspoon thyme
- 1/8 teaspoon salt and pepper as needed

Directions:

1. Take a large deep-frying pan and place it over medium-high heat
2. Add oil and let it heat up
3. Add chicken and cook for 4-5 minutes per side until slightly browned
4. Add spring onions and mushrooms, season with salt and pepper according to your taste
5. Stir
6. Cover with lid and bring the mix to a boil
7. Lower heat and simmer for 25 minutes
8. Serve!

Nutrition: Calories: 247 Fat: 12g Carbohydrates: 10g Protein: 23g

Chicken Breast Recipes

Note:

13. Blackened Chicken

Preparation Time: 10 minutes

Cooking Time: 10 minutes

Serving: 4

Ingredients:

- ½ teaspoon paprika
- 1/8 teaspoon salt

Chicken Breast Recipes

- ¼ teaspoon cayenne pepper
- ¼ teaspoon ground cumin
- ¼ teaspoon dried thyme
- 1/8 teaspoon ground white pepper
- 1/8 teaspoon onion powder
- 2 chicken breasts, boneless and skinless

Directions:

1. Preheat your oven to 350°F
2. Grease baking sheet
3. Take a cast-iron skillet and place it over high heat
4. Add oil and heat it up for 5 minutes until smoking hot
5. Take a small bowl and mix salt, paprika, cumin, white pepper, cayenne, thyme, onion powder
6. Oil the chicken breast on both sides and coat the breast with the spice mix
7. Transfer to your hot pan and cook for 1 minute per side
8. Transfer to your prepared baking sheet and bake for 5 minutes
9. Serve and enjoy!

Chicken Breast Recipes

Nutrition: Calories: 136 Fat: 3g Carbohydrates: 1g Protein: 24g

Chicken Breast Recipes

Note:

14. Grilled Chicken Salad

Preparation Time: 12 minutes

Cooking Time: 9 minutes

Serving: 4

Ingredients

- 4 boneless skinless chicken breasts
- 1 Tbsp (5 mL) soy sauce
- 2 tbsp (30 mL) extra virgin olive oil
- 2 tbsp (30 mL) cilantro, fresh, fresh
- 1 Tbsp (15 mL) ginger, minced
- 2 garlic cloves

Chicken Breast Recipes

- 1/2 tsp. (2.5 mL) hot pepper flakes
- 2 yellow bell pepper (s), large
- 3 tbsp (45 mL) rice vinegar
- 5 1/2 cups (1.375 L) mesclun salad

Directions:

1. Mince the cilantro or fresh cilantro. In a large bowl, combine the soy sauce, half the oil, cilantro, ginger and garlic. Add the chicken breasts and cover them well. Cover and marinate in the refrigerator for at least 30 minutes or up to a day.

2. Meanwhile, cut the peppers into quarters. Preheat the grill to medium heat. Grill the peppers for about 15 minutes. Pull out from the heat and place on a plate.

3. Place the chicken breasts on the greased grill and cook over medium heat 10 to 15 minutes per side or until a thermometer inserted into the breasts reads 165 ° F (74 ° C).

4. Slice grilled peppers and chicken into ½ inch wide strips. In a large salad bowl, mix chicken, peppers and salad. Add the rest of the oil and vinegar.

Nutrition 25g Protein 5g Carbohydrates 132mg Sodium 203mg Phosphorus 444mg Potassium

Chicken Breast Recipes

Note:

15. Chicken with Mushroom Sauce

Preparation Time: 9 minutes

Cooking Time: 36 minutes

Serving: 5

Ingredients

- 1/4 cup all-purpose flour
- 2 Tbsp light sour cream
- 1 tbsp Dijon mustard
- 1 cup chicken broth (use a salt-free brand)

Chicken Breast Recipes

- 4 chicken breasts (not "seasoned")
- 1/4 tsp. teaspoon dried thyme
- 1 tsp. 1 tablespoon non-hydrogenated margarine
- 1 1/2 cups mushrooms, quartered
- 3 green onions, chopped Ground
- 1/8 teaspoon pepper and chopped fresh parsley to taste

Directions:

1. Mix 2 tbsp flour, sour cream, mustard and 2 tbsp of chicken broth. Put aside. Sprinkle the breasts with thyme, pepper them and pass them in the flour.

2. Melt margarine in a large non-stick skillet over medium heat. Cook the breasts for about 5 minutes per side or until the poultry is no longer pink inside. Remove the breasts and keep them warm.

3. Place mushrooms to the pan and cook, stirring, for 3 minutes. Add the rest of the chicken broth, increase the heat and boil for 3 minutes.

4. Using a whisk, add the sour cream mixture; add the green onions. Stir until thickened (about 3

minutes). Pour over the chicken, season with pepper, garnish with parsley and serve.

Nutrition 25.4g Protein 5g Carbohydrates 99mg Sodium 205mg Phosphorus 289mg Potassium

Chicken Breast Recipes

Note:

16. Creamy Chicken with Cider

Preparation Time: 11 minutes

Cooking Time: 25 minutes

Serving: 8

Ingredients

- 4 bone-in chicken breasts
- 2 tbsp of lightly salted butter
- ¾ cup apple cider vinegar
- 2/3 cup of rich unsweetened coconut milk or cream

- 1/8 teaspoon kosher pepper

Directions:

1. Heat up butter in a skillet over medium heat.

2. Season the chicken with the pepper and add to the skillet. Cook over low heat for approx. 20 minutes.

3. Remove the chicken from the heat and set aside in a dish.

4. In the same skillet, add the cider and bring to a boil until most of it has evaporated.

5. Add the coconut cream and let cook for 1 minute until slightly thickened.

6. Pour the cider cream over the cooked chicken and serve.

Nutrition 87 Calories 1.88g Carbohydrate 94mg Sodium 74mg Potassium 36mg Phosphorus

Chicken Breast Recipes

Note:

17. Chicken Kebab Sandwich

Preparation Time: 15 minutes

Cooking Time: 15 minutes

Serving: 4

Ingredients

- 12 ounces boneless, skinless chicken breast
- 2 tablespoons freshly squeezed lemon juice
- 1 tablespoon extra-virgin olive oil
- 4 garlic cloves, minced, divided
- 1/8 teaspoon freshly ground black pepper
- ¼ cup plain, unsweetened yogurt
- 4 white flatbreads
- 1 cucumber, sliced

- 1 cup lettuce, shredded

Directions:

1. In a medium bowl, add the chicken breast, lemon juice, olive oil, and half the garlic, tossing to coat. Season with pepper. Set aside to marinate while you prepare the other ingredients.

2. In a small bowl, add the yogurt and remaining garlic. Season with pepper and mix well. Set aside.

3. Preheat skillet over medium-high heat and mix the chicken and the marinade. Cook for 5 minutes, until the chicken is well browned on the underside. Flip it over and cook the other side until the chicken is golden brown and the juices run clear. Remove from the pan and let rest for 5 minutes. Cut the chicken into thin slices.

4. In each flatbread, add some chicken, cucumber, and lettuce. Top with the yogurt sauce and serve.

Nutrition 22g Protein 217 Calories 231mg Potassium 80mg Phosphorus 339mg Sodium

Chicken Breast Recipes

Note:

18. Aromatic Chicken and Cabbage Stir-Fry

Preparation Time: 10 minutes

Cooking Time: 10 minutes

Serving: 4

Ingredients

- 1 teaspoon canola oil
- 10 ounces boneless, skinless chicken breast, thinly sliced
- 3 cups green cabbage, thinly sliced

Chicken Breast Recipes

- 1 tablespoon corn-starch
- 1 teaspoon ground ginger
- ½ teaspoon garlic powder
- ¼ cup water
- 1/8 teaspoon freshly ground black pepper

Directions:

1. With huge skillet over medium-high heat, heat the oil. Add the chicken and cook, stirring often, until browned and cooked through.

2. Cook cabbage to the pan for another 2 to 3 minutes

3. In a small bowl, mix the corn-starch, ginger, garlic, and water. Add the mixture to the pan, and continue cooking until the sauce has slightly thickened, about 1 minute. Season with pepper.

Nutrition 96 Calories 15g Protein 15mg Phosphorus 140mg Potassium 156mg Sodium

Chicken Breast Recipes

Note:

19. Thai-Style Chicken Curry

Preparation Time: 15 minutes

Cooking Time: 15 minutes

Serving: 4

Ingredients

For the curry paste

- 2 dried Thai red chilis
- 2 teaspoons coriander seeds
- 1 lemongrass stalk, outer layer removed, ends trimmed, tender green and white parts minced

Chicken Breast Recipes

- 1 shallot
- 4 garlic cloves
- 2-inch piece ginger, thinly sliced
- ½ cup fresh cilantro leaves and stems
- 1 teaspoon low-sodium soy sauce
- 2 tablespoons lime juice

For the curry

- 1 teaspoon canola oil
- 1-pound boneless, skinless chicken breast, thinly sliced
- 1 cup green beans, cut into 2-inch segments
- 1 cup water
- Juice of 1 lime
- 1 teaspoon brown sugar

Directions:

To make the curry paste

1. In a small bowl, add the chilis and cover with hot water. Leave to soak for 10 minutes.

2. Meanwhile, in a small, dry skillet, toast the coriander seeds until fragrant, shaking the pan

constantly to prevent burning. Transfer immediately to a food processor.

3. Drain the chilis and add them to the food processor, then add the lemongrass, shallot, garlic, ginger, cilantro, soy sauce, and lime juice. Grind into a fine paste, adding 1 or 2 tablespoons of water if needed. Use immediately, or transfer to an airtight container and store refrigerated for up to three days.

To make the curry

4. With a wok over medium-high heat, cook oil. Add the curry paste, and cook, stirring constantly, for about 30 seconds, until fragrant. Add the chicken breast and stir continuously until just browned.

5. Add the beans and 1 cup of water. Simmer for 5 minutes, until the chicken is cooked through, and the vegetables are tender.

6. Season with the lime juice and brown sugar. Serve over rice or rice noodles.

Nutrition 149 Calories 25g Protein 35mg Phosphorus 205mg Potassium 280mg Sodium

Chicken Breast Recipes

Note:

20. Chicken Satay with Peanut Sauce

Chicken Breast Recipes

Preparation Time: 2 hours

Cooking Time: 11 minutes

Serving: 6

Ingredients

For the chicken

- ½ cup plain, unsweetened yogurt
- 2 garlic cloves, minced
- 1-inch piece ginger, minced
- 2 teaspoons curry powder
- 1-pound boneless, skinless chicken breast, cut into strips
- 1 teaspoon canola oil

For the peanut sauce

- ¾ cup smooth unsalted peanut butter
- 1 teaspoon soy sauce
- 1 tablespoon brown sugar
- Juice of 2 limes
- ½ teaspoon red chili flakes
- ¼ cup hot water
- Fresh cilantro leaves, chopped, for garnish
- Lime wedges, for garnish

Directions:

To make the chicken

1. In a small bowl, add the yogurt, garlic, ginger, and curry powder. Stir to mix. Add the chicken strips to the marinade. Cover and refrigerate for 2 hours.

2. Thread the chicken pieces onto skewers.

3. Brush a grill pan with the oil, and heat on medium high. Cook the chicken skewers on each side for 3 to 5 minutes, until cooked through.

To make the peanut sauce

4. Using food processor, mix peanut butter, soy sauce, brown sugar, lime juice, red chili flakes, and hot water. Process until smooth. Transfer to a bowl, and sprinkle with the cilantro. Serve with the chicken satay along with lime wedges for squeezing over the skewers.

Nutrition 286 Calories 25g Protein 33mg Phosphorus 66mg Potassium 201mg Sodium

Chicken Breast Recipes

Note:

21. Chicken Breast and Bok Choy in Parchment

Preparation Time: 10 minutes

Cooking Time: 30 minutes

Serving: 4

Ingredients

- 1 tablespoon Dijon mustard
- 1 tablespoon extra-virgin olive oil
- 1 tablespoon chopped fresh thyme leaves
- 2 cups thinly sliced book choy

Chicken Breast Recipes

- 2 carrots, julienned
- 1 small leek, thinly sliced
- 4 boneless, skinless chicken breasts
- 1/8 teaspoon freshly ground black pepper
- 4 lemon slices

Directions:

1. Preheat the oven to 425°F.

2. Blend mustard, olive oil, and thyme.

3. Prepare four pieces of parchment paper by folding four 18-inch pieces in half and cutting them like you want to create a heart. Open each piece and lay flat.

4. In each piece of parchment, arrange ½ cup of book choy, a small handful of carrots, and a few slices of leek. Place the chicken breast on top, and season with pepper.

5. Brush the marinade over the chicken breasts, and top each with a slice of lemon.

6. Fold the packets shut and fold the paper along the edges to crease and seal the packages.

7. Cook for 20 minutes. Let rest for 5 minutes, and open carefully to serve.

Chicken Breast Recipes

Nutrition 164 Calories 24g Protein 26mg Phosphorus 187mg Potassium 356mg Sodium:

Chicken Breast Recipes

Note:

22. Chicken, Pasta, and Broccoli Bake

Preparation Time: 5 minutes

Cooking Time: 30 minutes

Serving: 6

Ingredients

- 8 ounces egg noodles

- 1 (10-ounce) package broccoli florets
- 2 tablespoons butter
- ½ sweet onion, chopped
- ¼ cup all-purpose flour
- 1½ cups Simple Chicken Broth or low-sodium store-bought chicken stock
- 1/8 teaspoon freshly ground black pepper
- ¾ cup Homemade Rice Milk or unsweetened store-bought rice milk
- 3 cups shredded cooked chicken breast
- ¼ cup shredded Cheddar cheese

Directions:

1. Preheat the oven to 350°F. Grease a 2-quart dish.

2. Boil water. Add the egg noodles and cook for 5 minutes. Add the broccoli and continue to cook for 3 to 5 more minutes, until the noodles are tender, and the broccoli is just fork-tender. Drain and set aside.

3. With a medium saucepan over medium-high heat, heat the butter. Add the onion and cook for 3 to 5 minutes, until it begins to soften. Add the flour and stir until evenly mixed. Add the broth and

season with pepper. Simmer for 5 minutes, until it begins to thicken. Add the rice milk and cook until heated through.

4. Toss the sauce with the broccoli, noodles, and cooked chicken, and transfer to the prepared baking dish. Top with the Cheddar cheese.

5. Bake for 20 minutes, uncovered, until browned and bubbly.

Nutrition 351 Calories 24g Protein 271mg Phosphorus 402mg Potassium 152mg Sodium

Chicken Breast Recipes

Note:

Chicken Breast Recipes

23. Chicken Pho

Preparation Time: 10 minutes

Cooking Time: 15 minutes

Serving: 4

Ingredients

- 5 cups Simple Chicken Broth or low-sodium store-bought chicken stock

- 1-inch piece ginger
- 1 cup cooked chicken breast
- ¼ cup Several fresh Thai basil sprigs
- 1 cup mung bean sprouts
- 1 lime
- 1 jalapeño pepper
- 1 (16-ounce) package dried rice vermicelli noodles
- 4 tablespoons (¼ cup) scallions
- 4 tablespoons (¼ cup) cilantro leaves

Directions:

1. Using a stockpot at medium-high heat, add the broth and ginger, and simmer. Mix in the chicken and simmer for 5 minutes. Remove the ginger from the pot and discard.

2. On a plate, place Thai basil, bean sprouts, lime wedges, and jalapeño slices.

3. Pour 1¼ cups of broth to each bowl. Garnish with 1 tablespoon each of the scallions and cilantro. Serve

Nutrition 325 Calories 21g Protein 205mg Phosphorus 389mg Potassium 313mg Sodium

Chicken Breast Recipes

Note:

24. Curried Chicken Stir-Fry

Preparation Time: 20 minutes

Cooking Time: 15 minutes

Servings: 6

Ingredients:

- 12 ounces of chicken breasts, 1-inch cubes, boneless skinless
- 2 teaspoons of curry powder
- 1/8 teaspoon of salt
- 1/8 teaspoon of freshly ground black pepper
- 1 (20-ounce) can of pineapple tidbits, strained, reserving juice

Chicken Breast Recipes

- 2 tablespoons of extra-virgin olive oil
- 1 yellow onion, chopped
- 2 red bell peppers, chopped

Directions:

1. In a medium bowl, toss the chicken, curry powder, salt, and pepper and set aside.

2. In a small saucepan, heat the reserved pineapple juice over low heat. Let it reduce, occasionally stirring, while you make the rest of the stir-fry.

3. Heat the large skillet with olive oil in medium heat. Add the chicken. Stir-fry for 3 for 4 minutes or until the chicken is light brown; it doesn't have to completely cook. Transfer the chicken to a plate.

4. Put the onion to the skillet and cook for 3 minutes, stirring, until the onion is crisp-tender. Check to make sure the pineapple liquid isn't burning and continue to stir it. Add bell peppers then stir-fry it for another 3 minutes, until crisp-tender.

5. Put the chicken back to the skillet, add the pineapple tidbits and cook, stirring, for 3 to 4 minutes or until the chicken is cooked through.

6. Add the thickened pineapple juice to the skillet and stir. Serve.

Nutrition: 215 Calories 98mg Sodium 146mg Phosphorus 374mg Potassium 19g Protein

Chicken Breast Recipes

Note:

25. Creamy Chicken

Preparation Time: 10 minutes

Cooking Time: 15 minutes

Servings: 2

Ingredients:

- 3 tbsp of unsalted butter
- 2 pounds of cut into 1-inch-thick strips skinless, boneless chicken breasts
- 4 minced garlic cloves
- ½ tsp. of ground ginger

- ½ tsp. of ground coriander
- ½ tsp. of ground cumin
- ¼ tsp. of crushed red pepper flakes
- ½ cup of chicken broth
- 1/3 cup of low-fat sour cream
- 1 tbsp of chopped fresh parsley

Directions:

1. Using skillet, warm up butter on medium-high heat.

2. Add chicken and cook for about 5–6 minutes.

3. Add garlic and spices and cook for 1 minute.

4. Add broth and bring to a boil. Reduce the heat to medium-low.

5. Simmer for about 5 minutes, stirring occasionally.

6. Stir in cream and simmer, occasionally stirring for about 3 minutes.

7. Serve hot with the garnishing of parsley.

Nutrition: 206 Calories 26.1g Protein 43mg Potassium 144mg Sodium

Chicken Breast Recipes

Note:

26. Fabulous Chicken

Preparation Time: 10 minutes

Cooking Time: 15 minutes

Servings: 8

Ingredients:

- 1 cup of low-sodium chicken broth
- 3 tbsp of balsamic vinegar
- 2 tsp. of corn-starch

- 2 tbsp of olive oil
- 4 minced garlic cloves
- 2 tbsp of minced fresh basil
- 4 (4-ounce) skinless, boneless chicken breasts
- Pinch of salt
- 1/8 teaspoon freshly ground black pepper, to taste
- 2 cored and sliced pears

Directions:

1. In a bowl, mix broth, vinegar, and cornstarch.
2. In a large skillet, heat oil on medium-high heat.
3. Add garlic and basil and sauté for about 1 minute.
4. Add chicken and sprinkle with salt and black pepper.
5. Cook for about 12–15 minutes. Transfer the chicken into a bowl.
6. In the same skillet, add pears and cook for about 4–5 minutes.

7. Add broth mixture and bring to a boil, cook for about 1 minute.

8. Reduce the heat to low.

9. Stir in chicken and cook for about 3–4 minutes.

Nutrition: 279 Calories 26.4g Protein 145mg Potassium 90mg Sodium

Chicken Breast Recipes

Note:

27. Chicken with Asian Vegetables

Preparation Time: 10 minutes

Cooking Time: 20 minutes

Servings: 8

Ingredients

- 2 tablespoons canola oil

Chicken Breast Recipes

- 6 boneless chicken breasts
- 1 cup low-sodium chicken broth
- 3 tablespoons reduced-sodium soy sauce
- ¼ teaspoon crushed red pepper flakes
- 1 garlic clove, crushed
- 1 can (8ounces) water chestnuts, sliced and rinsed (optional)
- ½ cup sliced green onions
- 1 cup chopped red or green bell pepper
- 1 cup chopped celery
- ¼ cup corn-starch
- 1/3 cup water
- 3 cups cooked white rice
- ½ large chicken breast for 1 chicken thigh

Directions:

1. Add warm oil in a skillet and dark-colored chicken on all sides.
2. Add chicken to a slow cooker with the remainder of the ingredients aside from corn-starch and water.
3. Spread and cook on low for 6 to 8 hours

4. Following 6–8 hours, independently blend corn-starch and cold water until smooth. Gradually include into the moderate cooker.

5. At that point, turn on high for about 15mins until thickened. Don't close the top on the moderate cooker to enable steam to leave.

6. Serve Asian blend over rice.

Nutrition: Calories: 415 Fat: 20g Protein: 20g Carbs: 36g

Chicken Breast Recipes

Note:

Printed by Libri Plureos GmbH in Hamburg, Germany